POCKET
prayers
for DADS

POCKET
prayers
for DADS

40 SIMPLE PRAYERS THAT BRING
STRENGTH AND FAITH

MAX LUCADO

WITH MARK MYNHEIR

THOMAS NELSON
Since 1798

Published in Nashville, Tennessee, by Thomas Nelson. Thomas Nelson is a registered trademark of HarperCollins Christian Publishing, Inc.

Thomas Nelson titles may be purchased in bulk for educational, business, fund-raising, or sales promotional use. For information, please e-mail SpecialMarkets@ThomasNelson.com.

Unless otherwise noted, Scripture quotations are taken from the New King James Version®. © 1982 by Thomas Nelson. Used by permission. All rights reserved.

Scripture quotations marked NCV are from the New Century Version®. © 2005 by Thomas Nelson. Used by permission. All rights reserved.

Scripture quotations marked NIV are from the Holy Bible, New International Version®, NIV®. Copyright © 1973, 1978, 1984, 2011 by Biblica, Inc.® Used by permission of Zondervan. All rights reserved worldwide. www.zondervan.com. The "NIV" and "New International Version" are trademarks registered in the United States Patent and Trademark Office by Biblica, Inc.®

Scripture quotations marked NLT are from the Holy Bible, New Living Translation. © 1996, 2004, 2007, 2013 by Tyndale House Foundation. Used by permission of Tyndale House Publishers, Inc., Carol Stream, Illinois 60188. All rights reserved.

Any Internet addresses, phone numbers, or company or product information printed in this book are offered as a resource and are not intended in any way to be or to imply an endorsement by Thomas Nelson, nor does Thomas Nelson vouch for the existence, content, or services of these sites, phone numbers, companies, or products beyond the life of this book.

ISBN 978-0-7180-7834-8 (eBook)

Library of Congress Control Number: 2015956802
ISBN 978-0-7180-7735-8

Printed in Mexico

16 17 18 19 20 RRD 10 9 8 7 6 5 4 3 2 1

The Pocket Prayer

Hello, my name is Max. I'm a recovering prayer wimp. I doze off when I pray. My thoughts zig, then zag, then zig again. Distractions swarm like gnats on a summer night. If attention deficit disorder applies to prayer, I am afflicted. When I pray, I think of a thousand things I need to do. I forget the one thing I set out to do: pray.

Some people excel in prayer. They inhale heaven and exhale God. They are the SEAL Team Six of intercession. They would rather pray than sleep. Why is it that I sleep when I pray? They belong to the PGA: Prayer Giants Association. I am a card-carrying member of the PWA: Prayer Wimps Anonymous.

Can you relate? It's not that we don't pray at all. We all pray some.

On tearstained pillows we pray.

In grand liturgies we pray.

At the sight of geese in flight, we pray.

Quoting ancient devotions, we pray.

We pray to stay sober, centered, or solvent. We pray when the lump is deemed malignant. When the money runs out before the month does. When the unborn baby hasn't kicked in a while. We all pray . . . some.

But wouldn't we all like to pray . . .

More?

Better?

Deeper?

Stronger?

With more fire, faith, or fervency?

Yet we have kids to feed, bills to pay, deadlines to meet.

The calendar pounces on our good intentions like a tiger on a rabbit. We want to pray, but *when*?

We want to pray, but *why*? We might as well admit it. Prayer is odd, peculiar. Speaking into space. Lifting words into the sky. We can't even get the cable company to answer us, yet God will? The doctor is too busy, but God isn't? We have our doubts about prayer.

And we have our checkered history with prayer: unmet expectations, unanswered requests. We can barely genuflect for the scar tissue on our knees. God, to some, is the ultimate heartbreaker. Why keep tossing the coins of our longings into a silent pool? He jilted me once . . . but not twice.

Oh, the peculiar puzzle of prayer.

We aren't the first to struggle. The sign-up sheet for Prayer 101 contains some familiar names: the apostles John, James, Andrew, and Peter. When one of Jesus' disciples requested, "Lord, teach us to pray" (Luke 11:1 NIV), none of the others objected. No one walked away saying, "Hey, I have prayer figured out." The first followers of Jesus needed prayer guidance.

In fact, the only tutorial they ever requested was on prayer. They could have asked for instructions on many topics: bread multiplying, speech making, storm stilling. Jesus raised people from the dead. But a "How to Vacate the Cemetery" seminar? His followers never called for one. But they did want him to do this: "Lord, teach us to pray."

The first followers of Jesus needed prayer guidance.

Might their interest have had something to do with the jaw-dropping, eye-popping promises Jesus attached to prayer? "Ask and it will be given to you" (Matt. 7:7 NIV). "If you believe, you will get anything you ask for in prayer" (Matt. 21:22 NCV). Jesus never attached such power to other endeavors. "*Plan* and it will be given to you." "You will get anything you *work* for." Those words are not in the Bible. But these are—"If you remain in me and follow my teachings, you can ask anything you want, and it will be given to you" (John 15:7 NCV).

Jesus gave stunning prayer promises.

And he set a compelling prayer example. Jesus prayed before he ate. He prayed for children. He prayed for the sick. He prayed with thanks. He prayed with tears. He had made the planets and shaped the stars, yet he prayed. He is the Lord of angels and Commander of heavenly hosts, yet he prayed. He is coequal with God, the exact representation of the Holy One, and yet he devoted himself to prayer. He prayed in the desert, cemetery, and garden. "He went out and departed to a solitary place; and there He prayed" (Mark 1:35).

This dialogue must have been common among his friends:

"Has anyone seen Jesus?"

"Oh, you know. He's up to the same thing."

"Praying *again*?"

"Yep. He's been gone since sunrise."

Jesus would even disappear for an entire night of prayer. I'm thinking of one occasion in particular. He'd just experienced one of the most stressful days of his ministry. The day began with the news of the death of his relative John the Baptist. Jesus sought to retreat with his disciples, yet a throng of thousands followed him. Though grief-stricken, he spent the day teaching and healing people. When it was discovered that the host of people had no food to eat, Jesus multiplied bread out of a basket and fed the entire multitude. In the span of a few hours, he battled sorrow, stress, demands, and needs. He deserved a good night's rest. Yet when evening finally came, he told the crowd to leave and the disciples to board their boat, and "he went up into the hills by himself to pray" (Mark 6:46 NLT).

Apparently it was the correct choice. A storm exploded over the Sea of Galilee, leaving the disciples "in trouble far away from land, for a strong wind had risen, and they were fighting heavy waves. About three o'clock in the morning Jesus came toward them, walking on the water" (Matt. 14:24–25 NLT). Jesus ascended the mountain depleted. He reappeared invigorated. When he reached the water, he never broke his stride. You'd have thought the water was a park lawn and the storm a spring breeze.

Do you think the disciples made the prayer–power connection? "Lord, teach us to pray *like that*. Teach us to find strength in prayer. To banish fear in prayer. To defy storms in prayer. To come off the mountain of prayer with the authority of a prince."

What about you? The disciples faced angry waves and a watery grave. You face angry clients, a turbulent economy, raging seas of stress and sorrow.

"Lord," we still request, "teach us to pray."

When the disciples asked Jesus to teach them to pray, he gave them a prayer. Not a lecture on prayer. Not the doctrine of prayer. He gave them a quotable, repeatable, portable prayer (Luke 11:1–4).

Could you use the same? It seems to me that the prayers of the Bible can be distilled into one. The result is a simple, easy-to-remember, pocket-size prayer:

Father,
> *you are good.*
>> *I need help. Heal me and forgive me.*
>>> *They need help.*
>>>> *Thank you.*
>>>>> *In Jesus' name, amen.*

Let this prayer punctuate your day. As you begin your morning, *Father, you are good.* As you commute to work or walk the hallways at school, *I need help.* As you wait in the grocery line, *They need help.* Keep this prayer in your pocket as you pass through the day.

When we invite God into our world, he walks in. He brings

a host of gifts: joy, patience, resilience. Anxieties come, but they don't stick. Fears surface and then depart. Regrets land on the windshield, but then comes the wiper of prayer. The devil still hands me stones of guilt, but I turn and give them to Christ. I'm completing my sixth decade, yet I'm wired with energy. I am happier, healthier, and more hopeful than I have ever been. Struggles come, for sure. But so does God.

Prayer is not a privilege for the pious, not the art of a chosen few. Prayer is simply a heartfelt conversation between God and his child.

Prayer is not a privilege for the pious, not the art of a chosen few. Prayer is simply a heartfelt conversation between God and his child. My friend, he wants to talk with you. Even now, as you read these words, he taps at the door. Open it. Welcome him in. Let the conversation begin.

Prayers for Faith
and Family

1

The name of the LORD is a strong tower;
the righteous run to it and are safe.

PROVERBS 18:10

Dear Lord, you are the strong tower, the mighty fortress for your people. No one can stand against you.

Remind me to run to you daily. All too often I rely on my own strength and think I'm the only one who can protect my family and keep them from difficult situations. I can't. Only you can. Help me have the faith to trust you for our protection and care.

As my family walks through this day, they need the physical and spiritual protection only you can provide. Please be the strong tower for them and guide them so they will not try to rely on themselves but on you alone.

Thank you, Lord, for being my protector and shield in times of trouble.

In your precious name I pray, amen.

2

I have been crucified with Christ; it is no longer I who live, but Christ lives in me; and the life which I now live in the flesh I live by faith in the Son of God, who loved me and gave Himself for me.

GALATIANS 2:20

Heavenly Father, you are gracious and merciful. Only by your love and your Son's sacrifice on the cross am I saved.

I need your help to fully understand this truth and live it out in my life. I want to follow you and never forget or take for granted that you gave your Son's life for mine. Help me each day to die a little more to the things that keep me from a right relationship with you. Help me walk in faith and set the example for my family.

Bless my family today. Help them live by faith and set their eyes on you alone for their salvation. Guide my children's hearts so they will walk with you every day.

Thank you for caring for me and my family and for the precious gift of your Son.

In Jesus' holy name, amen.

3

---

*He said, "Come." And when Peter had come
down out of the boat, he walked on the water
to go to Jesus. But when he saw that the wind
was boisterous, he was afraid; and beginning
to sink he cried out, saying, "Lord, save me!"*

MATTHEW 14:29-30

Almighty God, you are in control of all things. Even the power of nature rests squarely in your hands.

Many times I am just like Peter. I start out with good intentions to follow you but quickly get frightened or discouraged, and my faith wavers. I want to follow you without faltering, with power and confidence in you and your plan for my life. Strengthen my faith. Please guide me so that when the storms of life come, I will keep my eyes and my heart focused on you, and I will not fear or doubt.

I ask you to be with my family today through the storms, whether big or small. Teach them to look to you constantly and not to waver. Bless my home with the peace only you can bring.

Thank you for lifting us up in times of trouble and pain.

In your Son's name, amen.

4

I know what it is to be in need, and I know what it is to have plenty. I have learned the secret of being content in any and every situation, whether well fed or hungry, whether living in plenty or in want. I can do all this through him who gives me strength.

PHILIPPIANS 4:12-13 NIV

Father, you control our every circumstance, our every breath. Your power and majesty know no limits.

I sometimes struggle with being satisfied in my life. I find myself complaining about one thing or another, desiring what I don't have instead of being content with what I do have. Please heal me of this, and help me find true contentment in you and in the blessings you have given me.

Help my family not to chase after the things culture says they need in order to be fulfilled. Give them strength to resist the pull of the world. Guide the hearts of my family today that they will find their satisfaction in you alone.

Thank you for quenching our spiritual thirst and comforting our souls.

In Christ's name, amen.

5

---

*In everything give thanks; for this is the
will of God in Christ Jesus for you.*

1 Thessalonians 5:18

Dear God, by your mighty word you can move mountains and create life. And yet, in your magnificent glory you still know me by name and watch carefully over me and my family.

Remind me today, Father, to give thanks for everything you do. I owe my life and my every breath to you. I find it so easy to walk through my day and take for granted all the miracles and gifts in my life. Please forgive me. Change my heart and my attitude.

Give my family a spirit of thankfulness today. Help them see the multitude of reasons they have to thank you in this day you have made.

Thank you, Lord, for my life and my family. Thank you for joy, peace, and provision. Thank you that we can tell others about you. And thank you for loving us.

In Jesus' name, amen.

6

They are no longer two but one flesh.
Therefore what God has joined
together, let not man separate.

MATTHEW 19:6

Heavenly Father, no evil can stand against you. The schemes of the Enemy have no power in your awesome presence. You are a shield and a rock for your people.

Protect my marriage. I am constantly bombarded with temptations, and there always seems to be some new wedge trying to force its way between my wife and me. Please pour out your love on our marriage so our promises to each other and to you remain unbroken. Keep the Enemy from getting strongholds in our relationship. Help me use my words and actions to strengthen our bond and never harm it.

Bless my wife today. Protect her, encourage her, and wrap your love around her. Help her focus on our relationship with each other and with you.

Thank you for my marriage. Thank you for caring about it more than I ever could. Thank you for giving me the strength to honor and cherish my wife.

In your Son's name, amen.

7

---

*Who can find a virtuous wife? For
her worth is far above rubies.*

PROVERBS 31:10

Almighty Father, you are just and holy, the mighty God, the Eternal One.

Help me appreciate my wife more. She carries so much on her shoulders. She keeps our family going when I'm away, and she blesses me immensely when I'm home. I fear that I don't give her the love and respect I should. Please, Lord, grant me the heart to honor my wife and to show her and tell her how much she means to me and our family. Help me be the husband she needs, desires, and deserves.

Please guide my children today to appreciate their mother and surround her with love and encouragement. Lift my wife's spirits, and let her know how much she means to our family.

Thank you for the wonderful wife you have given me. She is truly a precious gift from you.

In Jesus' holy name, amen.

Prayers for Courage and Strength

8

I am not ashamed of the gospel of Christ, for it is the power of God to salvation for everyone who believes.

ROMANS 1:16

L ord, by your name alone are people saved. Your unfailing love built the bridge from you to us. Your love conquers all.

Help me be bold with my faith and unashamed that I follow you so I will speak freely about you. Help me walk in courage and faith every day because my strength and dependence flow from the Holy Spirit. Provide opportunities for me to share your love with my friends and coworkers, and give me the heart to stand strong for you. Teach me how to be an example for my children.

Bless my family, Lord, so they will know you and will want to tell others about you. Give them an excitement and a deep joy in serving you. Fill our home with your strength and courage.

Thank you for strengthening our hearts and our resolve to follow you without apprehension or wavering.

In your Son's name, amen.

9

The Lord is near to all who call upon
Him, to all who call upon Him in truth.

PSALM 145:18

Dear God, you are the Alpha and Omega, the beginning and the end of all things. You are worthy of all praise and honor.

Even though sometimes I feel so far away from you, help me know that you are always right here beside me. And help me to call on you in truth and to seek you with my whole heart. I'm thankful I'm not walking through this life without you.

Draw my family close to you today so they can feel your presence. Help my children learn to call on you always. Teach them to pray more and to rely on you.

Thank you for choosing to be with your creation and for loving us so much. I praise you for desiring a relationship with us.

In Jesus' name, amen.

10

---

*The Lord is my light and my salvation;
whom shall I fear? The Lord is the strength
of my life; of whom shall I be afraid?*

Psalm 27:1

Father, you are the light of the world and the hope of all people. You strengthen those who follow you. You are our hope and our salvation!

Calm my fears and worries today. Help me stay focused on you and what's important in my life. I get caught up in worrying about small things that really don't matter, especially in view of your salvation. Help me rest in your promises and just trust you.

Light the way for my wife and children today. When they start to fret over daily concerns, remind them that you love them and watch over them at all times.

Thank you for keeping fear and worry from having a choke hold on our lives. I am so thankful you care about the small things as well as the large ones.

In your Son's name, amen.

11

"Not by might nor by power, but by My Spirit," says the LORD of hosts.

ZECHARIAH 4:6

Father, by your Spirit the world was created and is sustained. By your Spirit you lead and guide your people. I praise your holy name.

As I face obstacles, fears, and temptations, please guide me to rely on you. Point me to scriptures that will give me the courage and strength to face the day. Give me a humble attitude so I will simply listen to you and follow your leading.

Direct my wife and children today. Show them your loving grace and wisdom. Protect them and give them peace as they learn to rely on you and not themselves.

Thank you for sending your Spirit to lead, comfort, and protect us. Thank you for loving my family more than I ever could.

In Jesus' name, amen.

12

*I have told you these things, so that
in me you may have peace. In this
world you will have trouble. But take
heart! I have overcome the world.*

JOHN 16:33 NIV

God, your peace surpasses all understanding, and your mercies are new every morning. Your majesty flows over all the earth.

Today I feel as if my troubles are about to overwhelm me. The world seems to be pressing in on all sides, and I feel trapped by worry and fear. Help me have your peace and your assurance that you have already overcome all my concerns. Forgive me for not trusting you as I should. Steady my faith.

Walk closely with my family today. Keep my children from being apprehensive or saddened by the obstacles in their lives. Wrap your arms around them, and calm their hearts so they aren't overcome by anxiety or dread.

Thank you that you have already defeated any future troubles so I don't have to be afraid. I am extremely thankful for the encouragement of your promises.

In your Son's name, amen.

13

And we know that all things work together
for good to those who love God, to those who
are the called according to His purpose.

ROMANS 8:28

Dear God, you are great and mighty. You planned and purposed every moment of every life on earth. You know all and control all. You are Lord of all!

Remind me today that when unexpected, troublesome, or even painful things enter my life, you have allowed them for my benefit—to strengthen me. Help me to appreciate the difficulties and challenges and to have the proper attitude toward them.

As my children learn more about you and your ways, help them realize you want only good for them. Teach them to pray and walk with you through the good times and bad. Reinforce their faith today.

Thank you for weaving the events and circumstances in our lives to fit in your amazing plan. I am grateful that your plan includes my family.

In Christ's name, amen.

14

---

*As for me and my house, we
will serve the LORD.*

JOSHUA 24:15

L ord, you are all-knowing and all-powerful. Heaven is your throne, and the earth is your footstool.

I wonder sometimes if I'm teaching my family about you like I should. Guide me to be a godly man so I can be the kind of father and husband you want me to be. Break down any barriers that keep me from being that man.

Show my children and my family that your ways are best. Create in them the desire to follow you so they will love you with all their hearts, all their minds, and all their souls.

I am so grateful I can come to you on behalf of my family. Thank you for carefully watching over them and leading them to you.

In your holy name, amen.

Prayers for Leadership and Wisdom

15

Jesus, knowing that the Father had given all things into His hands, and that He had come from God and was going to God, rose from supper and laid aside His garments, took a towel and girded Himself. After that, He poured water into a basin and began to wash the disciples' feet, and to wipe them with the towel with which He was girded.

JOHN 13:3-5

Lord, despite having all the power and majesty of God, you still chose to be with your creation and even to serve us. Your love, mercy, and grace are beyond comprehension.

When I think of leading my family or others, please remind me of this scripture. Give me the heart of a servant leader. Humble my spirit so I will desire to serve as you served, to lead as you led. Keep me from thinking too highly of myself.

Let your humility pour onto my children, and guide them with your example. Don't let them become too focused on themselves and their wants and desires.

Thank you that you are so powerful and yet so gentle with your people. I am grateful that you show yourself to us in many different ways.

In Jesus' name, amen.

16

Show me Your ways, O Lord; teach me Your paths. Lead me in Your truth and teach me, for You are the God of my salvation; on You I wait all the day.

PSALM 25:4–5

God, your ways are wise and true. Your decrees breathe life into your people. You are a God who forever directs their steps.

I confess that I have not studied your Word as much as I should. I want to know you more and be led by you. I want to guide my family and run my home by your loving instructions. Give me the discipline to study your Word and the ears to hear your voice. Show me, Lord.

Open my children's eyes to you today. They are growing quickly. Before too long they will be off to college or on their own. Please capture their hearts now and walk with them through the rest of their lives.

Thank you for giving us your Word so we may know you. Thank you for protecting us from ourselves with your instructions.

In your holy name, amen.

17

---

*Trust in the LORD with all your heart, and
lean not on your own understanding;
in all your ways acknowledge Him,
and He shall direct your paths.*

PROVERBS 3:5-6

Heavenly Father, you are the same today, tomorrow, and forever. Your loving character and holiness are unchangeable.

I really struggle with trusting you in every aspect of my life. I constantly want to take control and work things out myself. Forgive me. Help me acknowledge you first and to look for your direction. I want to have your insight and wisdom in all I do.

Bless my wife and children today. As our family praises you together, direct our lives. Blaze a careful path for each of my children, and guide them along that path to you. Teach my wife to rely on you for all things.

I am so grateful for the wife and children you have given me. Thank you for your constant desire to gently direct our way.

In Christ's name, amen.

18

---

*Do I now persuade men, or God? Or do I
seek to please men? For if I still pleased men,
I would not be a bondservant of Christ.*

GALATIANS 1:10

Almighty God, you hear my cries and comfort me. Your loving grace has wrapped itself around my heart. I am so blessed to be your child.

Sometimes I worry more about what people think than what your Word tells me. I often feel as if my feet are planted in two separate worlds. Please forgive me and help me be more obedient to you. Guide me to walk in your ways without shame or wavering. Help me be bold for you and the truth of your Word.

Infuse my family with faith and confidence. Clear out the distractions and obstacles in our home that hinder your work there. Help us set the right priorities, and teach us not to compromise on your Word and what we know to be true.

Thank you for your patience and grace. I am so grateful for the incredible blessings you have given our family.

In Jesus' holy name, amen.

19

*Shepherd the flock of God which is among you,
serving as overseers, not by compulsion but
willingly, not for dishonest gain but eagerly;
nor as being lords over those entrusted to you,
but being examples to the flock; and when
the Chief Shepherd appears, you will receive
the crown of glory that does not fade away.*

1 PETER 5:2-4

God, your righteous love drives away fear and sin. Your thoughts and will are always for our good. You are the true and perfect Father.

I want to be the father to my children and the husband to my wife that you created me to be. Help me guide my family by your Word so I can shepherd my family gently and with wisdom. Keep me from my selfish desires and foolish decisions.

Direct our children as they go through their days. Keep your angels near them. Stir their hearts to love one another and to be kind to others. Help them appreciate the blessings of our family.

Thank you for teaching me how to be the head of my family. I am grateful I have your Word and your Spirit to guide me.

In your name, amen.

20

If any of you lacks wisdom, let him ask of God, who gives to all liberally and without reproach, and it will be given to him.

JAMES 1:5

Heavenly Father, you have the power to bring life out of death. You breathe your very Spirit into us. You are the one and only true God.

Lord, I am asking you to bless me with this promise. I am humbly seeking your wisdom to lead my family, guide my life, and direct my career. I am also asking that you give me the understanding to serve you with all my heart, mind, strength, and talents.

My wife and children desire your wisdom and guidance for their lives too. Bless them with your knowledge and grace today.

Thank you for loving us so much that you're willing to teach us everything we need to know. Thank you for being so generous with your knowledge and wisdom.

In Jesus' name, amen.

Prayers for Patience and Balance

21

Wait on the LORD; be of good courage,
and He shall strengthen your heart;
wait, I say, on the LORD!

PSALM 27:14

Heavenly Father, you are slow to anger and compassionate and long-suffering. Your timing is perfect, and your ways are right.

Forgive me for being impatient and lacking the faith that you are guiding my steps. Give me peace in my heart to be content with your timing and your direction in all areas of my life. Help me subdue my desire to control all things, and instead teach me to wait for and listen to your voice.

Bring a calm spirit to our home today, and let my family rest in your gentle care. May my children take small, steady steps toward a mature faith.

Thank you for doing what is best for us in your timing, not ours, as you watch over our lives.

In Jesus' name, amen.

22

I know the thoughts that I think toward you, says the Lord, thoughts of peace and not of evil, to give you a future and a hope.

Jeremiah 29:11

Lord, you spoke the foundations of the earth and all the heavens into existence. You are eternal and unchanging. You are the magnificent Creator!

There are days when hope feels very far away, when it seems as if nothing matters and everything is out of control. Help me fight these feelings and rely instead on what you have promised—that you have a plan for me and it is good.

Remind my family today that you have a plan for all of us. Comfort them with the knowledge that you are in control and everything you do is for our good. Soothe my wife's spirit, and let us be united as we seek your will for our family.

Thank you for restoring our hope. I am grateful that you care enough for us to hold our future in your hands.

In your Son's name, amen.

23

But those who wait on the LORD shall renew their strength; they shall mount up with wings like eagles, they shall run and not be weary, they shall walk and not faint.

ISAIAH 40:31

My Father in heaven, you are immeasurably capable of doing whatever we ask or imagine. You are worthy of all glory and honor.

I need you. Most days I feel drained of strength and desire. I try to be a good father, husband, and Christian, but I get worn down. Please renew my strength. Restore the energy and passion I had when I first followed you, and give me the desire to live the life you have for me.

The hectic pace of life seems to overrun our family at times. There's always somewhere to be or something to do. Even church functions and serving others can get exhausting. Refresh my family so we can better serve you and others.

You are our source of strength in chaotic times. Thank you for being our ever-present help.

In Christ's name, amen.

24

To everything there is a season, a time
for every purpose under heaven.

ECCLESIASTES 3:1

Father, many are the wonders you have done, and magnificent are your plans. You are great and do marvelous things!

I feel torn at times, and it seems my life gets off track. Teach me to keep my relationship with you and my responsibilities to my family as my first and foremost priorities. Help me to keep order in my life and to manage my time and treasures appropriately.

Transform my family and how we look at our schedules. We get so busy and often spend our time and attention on things that won't last. Bring stability and balance to our home.

Thank you for every season of life. I am so grateful that you want us to enjoy all the blessings you have given us.

In Jesus' holy name, amen.

25

He said to them, "Come aside by yourselves
to a deserted place and rest a while."

MARK 6:31

Dear Lord, your rest is a blessing to all who call on your name. You are the shelter and the comfort during the storms. You are the great I AM.

I am exhausted. I run myself ragged with working, taking care of my family, and trying to fulfill my obligations. Show me how to take a Sabbath and rest my body, mind, and soul so I might serve you better and be the coworker and father and husband I want to be.

Remind my family what it means to slow down and take a break. Show them it is okay to take time away and rejuvenate, and help them use that time to focus on you and the life you have for them.

Thank you for not only giving us permission to rest but also showing us how.

In your name, amen.

26

---

*Whatever things are true, whatever things
are noble, whatever things are just, whatever
things are pure, whatever things are lovely,
whatever things are of good report, if
there is any virtue and if there is anything
praiseworthy—meditate on these things.*

PHILIPPIANS 4:8

Heavenly Father, you are the source of all that is beautiful and good. You are the wellspring of life and all that exists. Your name is worthy of all praise and honor.

I get too caught up in the negative and depressing aspects of this world, and my mind strays from you. Help me focus on the positive and good things you provide. When I drift into the negative, remind me to refocus on your character traits, and let my children see in me your positive qualities.

Keep the evil one from distorting my children's view of your world. Regardless of the circumstances, may they always see the beauty of your hand in their lives.

Thank you for pouring out the magnificence of your character on our world. I am grateful you have given us eyes to see your work.

In Christ's name, amen.

27

---

*Where your treasure is, there
your heart will be also.*

MATTHEW 6:21

Father, your Son is the greatest treasure from heaven. He is the ultimate gift and the mighty Savior. His name will be praised forever.

In my heart I put things above you and your will. Please forgive me. Restore my desire to place you, your wisdom, and your guidance for my life above all else. Let my treasures not be the things of this world but the good gifts you have for me.

The hearts of my children are still growing and learning. Don't let them be snared by the trappings of this world. Please gently guide them to focus on your good will for their lives. Keep their priorities straight, and help me raise them.

Thank you for clearing out the clutter of our lives and turning our attention back to you. Thank you for all your wonderful blessings.

In your Son's name, amen.

Prayers for Holiness and Integrity

28

No temptation has overtaken you except such as is common to man; but God is faithful, who will not allow you to be tempted beyond what you are able, but with the temptation will also make the way of escape, that you may be able to bear it.

1 Corinthians 10:13

Heavenly Father, you are faithful and just. You keep your promises of love for a thousand generations. I will follow you always.

Temptation waits for me around every corner. Because of the television, the computer, and my own sinful heart, I struggle with desires to look at things or to act in ways I know are contrary to your will. Please forgive me and strengthen me to face those battles. When temptations come, help me have the wisdom and strength to avoid them. Place your Word in my heart so I will strive to live for you.

Protect my wife and children today. So many things vie for their attention. Keep the schemes of the evil one from them, and let their desires always be to please you.

Thank you for your promise to help us with our temptations and struggles. I am grateful you have given us scriptures to guide us.

In Jesus' name, amen.

29

Blessed is the man who fears the LORD, who delights greatly in His commandments. His descendants will be mighty on earth; the generation of the upright will be blessed.

PSALM 112:1-2

Almighty Lord, the depth of your wisdom knows no end. The magnitude of your plans is immeasurable. Great and mighty are you!

Help me be fully committed to your words and commandments. Fill me with the Holy Spirit and the desire to do your will at all times. Guide me to be a godly man of integrity so I will live for you, and my children will know your blessings.

I earnestly want my children to have a strong relationship with you, to follow you out of love and reverence all their days. Have mercy on them, and give them your grace to know you.

Thank you for giving us the power to follow you even when we don't think we can. I am grateful for the Holy Spirit, who gently guides me.

In your Son's name, amen.

30

*Flee also youthful lusts; but pursue
righteousness, faith, love, peace with those
who call on the Lord out of a pure heart.*

2 TIMOTHY 2:22

God, you assemble your people from all around the world. You are the Good Shepherd, who gathers and protects his flock.

Help me win the battle against lust. I struggle with habits and thoughts I know you don't want me to engage in. At times I feel powerless. Guide me to a strong Christian brother to whom I can be accountable. Help me have victory over this battle.

Protect my home and my family from destructive forces. Keep my children safe and guard their hearts. Give my wife and me wisdom on how to make our home a pure and secure place.

I am thankful you have given us a community of believers who help and encourage one another. Thank you that, because of that community and your faithful presence, I am not alone in this.

In Jesus' name, amen.

31

*In all things showing yourself to be a
pattern of good works; in doctrine showing
integrity, reverence, incorruptibility, sound
speech that cannot be condemned, that
one who is an opponent may be ashamed,
having nothing evil to say of you.*

TITUS 2:7–8

Father, you do not treat your people as they deserve, but you are gracious and merciful, patient and forgiving. I am humbled by your amazing pardon of all our sins.

Let your integrity and character flow through me. So many people I know and work with don't know you. Help me keep my behavior consistent with being a Christian so they might see you through me. Provide opportunities to share your love with those around me.

Instill in my family your thoughts and wishes. May we always keep them at the forefront of our home. Guide my wife and children to seek your plan for their lives, and be with them today as they go their separate ways.

Thank you for showing us what is right in your sight.

In Jesus' name, amen.

32

---

*If it is possible, as much as depends on
you, live peaceably with all men.*

ROMANS 12:18

Almighty God, we will celebrate the abundance of your goodness and will shout for joy because of your overflowing grace.

Keep me from the petty conflicts that can interrupt my life and don't reflect well on you. Help me be a peacemaker. Show me the people I need to go to and heal a division. Empower me to walk in integrity for your name's sake.

Bless our marriage by removing any conflicts between my wife and me, and keep the evil one from stirring up tension and strife. Teach us both to rely on you and your instruction. Place your calming spirit in our home.

I am grateful you show us the way that is good and true. Thank you for being the Prince of Peace.

In Christ's name, amen.

33

Let your conduct be without covetousness;
be content with such things as you have.

HEBREWS 13:5

Lord, your law is perfect and converts the soul. Your testimony is pure and wise. You are the defender of all who trust in you.

I am bombarded with messages every day that say I need more things to make me happy and satisfied. Help me not to listen to those messages or to be preoccupied by what others have. Teach me to find my fulfillment in you, not in bigger houses and more toys. Show me what true contentment is.

Please help my wife and me to be united in how we manage our money and resources. Remind us to be open and honest with each other in this area. Keep our desires in check so we're not chasing after the next best thing. Instead, fill our family with thanksgiving and satisfaction.

Thank you for providing all we truly need and teaching us what we don't need. Thank you for being the source of balance in a hectic world.

In Jesus' holy name, amen.

34

Create in me a clean heart, O God, and
renew a steadfast spirit within me.

PSALM 51:10

Our Father in heaven, you are the great Redeemer. You reached down from heaven and saved humanity by your own mighty hand. Your love can never be matched.

I feel overwhelmed and ashamed by my sin. As much as I struggle and fight, I still stumble and fall far too often. Please forgive me. You know my heart better than I do. Cleanse me and renew me so I have a fresh spirit to serve you.

Remind my family today that you are the God who restores souls and heals wounds. Teach them never to be afraid to approach you and ask for forgiveness.

Thank you for taking pleasure in reconciling your people. I am so grateful to serve a God who continues to love us regardless of how many times we mess up.

In your Son's name, amen.

Prayers for Fatherhood and Joy

35

---

*Behold, children are a heritage from the
LORD, the fruit of the womb is a reward.*

PSALM 127:3

A lmighty God, your love is immeasurable. Your love is so great that you sent your one and only Son to die for me and my family.

I have so many worries about my children and whether or not I'm a good father to them. I love them so much and want the very best for them, but I often doubt myself and my parenting skills. Grant me your peace as I strive to do my best, and give me the wisdom, discernment, and confidence to make the right decisions for them.

Be with my wife today as she guides and loves our children. Give her the patience and insight she needs to get our family through this day.

Thank you for the incredible joy of being my children's father. Thank you for loving my children more than I ever could.

In Christ's name I pray, amen.

36

These words which I command you today shall be in your heart. You shall teach them diligently to your children, and shall talk of them when you sit in your house, when you walk by the way, when you lie down, and when you rise up.

<small>DEUTERONOMY 6:6-7</small>

God, you are the maker of heaven and earth, the all-powerful Creator. You are worthy of all praise and honor.

Fill me with your Spirit and your mind. Help me communicate your words and commands to my children. Guide my thoughts and our conversations so that, as a family, we will talk more about you and learn more about you. Teach me to be a godly example for my children so they will be encouraged to follow you.

Reach down and touch my children's hearts, Lord. Open their ears and their hearts to your words and your heart, and remove any barriers that the evil one puts in their way.

Thank you for my children's love and for allowing me to raise them. I am grateful for the opportunity to tell them about you.

In Jesus' name, amen.

37

A soft answer turns away wrath,
but a harsh word stirs up anger.

PROVERBS 15:1

Heavenly Father, you speak to us in gentle whispers, and yet your words carry the power of eternal life. I am in awe of your mighty ways.

Sometimes I say things to my children I later regret. Remind me of the impact my words have on them. Forgive me and heal any wounds I have caused. Guide my thoughts and words so I will encourage my children and not tear them down. Soften my heart and how I express myself.

Lift my children's spirits today. Bless them with your encouragement, and build them up by giving them a joy and a reverence for you. Let kindness and gentleness flow through our home.

Thank you for taming my tongue and giving me a desire to gently cultivate my children's spirits. I am so grateful you have given these children to me.

In your Son's name, amen.

38

---

*Be kind to one another, tenderhearted,
forgiving one another, even as
God in Christ forgave you.*

EPHESIANS 4:32

Father, you are a loving and forgiving God. You are our advocate and our redeemer. You deal righteously and compassionately with your people.

Teach me to forgive as you do and to model that kind of grace and mercy for my wife and children. Help me be the kind of father that my family can always come to without fearing my reaction. Strengthen our love for each other and you.

Work in my children's hearts to have the spirit of repentance. Help us be open and honest in our relationships, and guide us to follow your example when we are wronged or hurt.

I am grateful for your grace and mercy in our lives. Thank you for drawing us to you and making true forgiveness possible.

In Jesus' name, amen.

39

*Now may the God of hope fill you with all joy
and peace in believing, that you may abound
in hope by the power of the Holy Spirit.*

Romans 15:13

Heavenly Father, you turn our sorrows into dancing and our defeats into celebrations. You are the God who refreshes his people.

Even though I have many reasons to be jubilant and appreciative, I focus too often on the negative and dark things in my life. Fill me again with your joy and peace and an appreciation for your blessings. Teach me how to have fun and take pleasure in the life you have given me.

My family needs your constant presence. When my children are older, let them remember that our home was filled with happiness and laughter. Give them eyes to search for joy regardless of their circumstances.

Thank you for the gift of joy and happiness and all the pleasures associated with being your child.

In Jesus' name, amen.

40

Rejoice in the Lord always.
Again I will say, rejoice!

PHILIPPIANS 4:4

Lord, you are the God of heaven and earth. You see from the beginning to the end and have made us to be with you for eternity. May we forever praise your name!

I want to remain focused on you and the pleasure of knowing that I will be with you always. Don't let the evil one cloud my thoughts and steal the sheer joy of being one of your children. Keep my eyes and thoughts on the eternity I will spend with you.

Walk with my family today and always. Teach them to appreciate and enjoy your many blessings. Remind them that they belong to you forever.

Thank you for saving me and loving my family. Thank you for pouring your Spirit into us and giving us a tiny glimpse now of what it will be like with you in heaven.

In Christ's name, amen.

About Max Lucado

More than 120 million readers have found inspiration and encouragement in the writings of Max Lucado. He lives with his wife, Denalyn, and their mischievous mutt, Andy, in San Antonio, Texas, where he serves the people of Oak Hills Church. Visit his website at MaxLucado.com or follow him at Twitter.com/MaxLucado and Facebook.com/MaxLucado.

About Mark Mynheir

Mark Mynheir is a former Marine and a career police officer, who has served as a narcotics agent, a S.W.A.T. Team member, and a homicide detective. Mark also divides his time as an author, having published five novels and multiple magazine articles (www.copwriter.com). He has been married for more than twenty-five years to the love of his life, Lori, and they have three fantastic children—Chris, Shannon, and Justin.

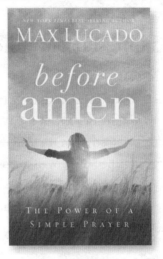

Make Your Prayers Personal

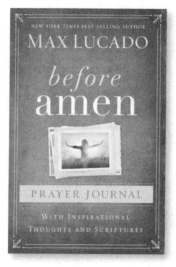

ISBN 978-0-7180-1406-3

$13.99

This beautiful companion journal to *Before Amen* helps readers stoke their prayer life. It features quotes and scriptures to inspire both prayer warriors and those who struggle to pray.

Tools for Your Church and Small Group

Before Amen: A DVD Study

ISBN 978-0-529-12342-8

$21.99

Max Lucado leads this four-session study through his discovery of a simple tool for connecting with God each day. This study will help small-group participants build their prayer life, calm the chaos of their world, and grow in Christ.

Before Amen Study Guide

ISBN 978-0-529-12334-3

$9.99

This guide is filled with Scripture study, discussion questions, and practical ideas designed to help small-group members understand Jesus' teaching on prayer. An integral part of the *Before Amen* small-group study, it will help group members build prayer into their everyday lives.

Before Amen
Church Campaign Kit

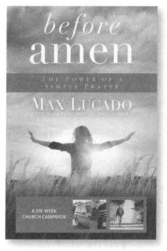

ISBN 978-0-529-12369-5

$49.99

The church campaign kit includes a four-session DVD study by Max Lucado; a study guide with discussion questions and video notes; the *Before Amen* trade book; a getting started guide; and access to a website with all the sermon resources churches need to launch and sustain a four-week *Before Amen* campaign.

Before Amen for Everyone

Before Amen Audiobook

ISBN 978-1-4915-4662-8 | $19.99

Enjoy the unabridged audio CD of *Before Amen*.

Before Amen eBook

ISBN 978-0-529-12390-9

Read *Before Amen* anywhere on your favorite tablet or electronic device.

Antes del amén Spanish Edition

ISBN 978-0-7180-0157-5 | $13.99

The hope of *Before Amen* is also available for Spanish-language readers.